Translations of Christian Literature
Series III—Liturgical Texts

COPTIC OFFICES

COPTIC OFFICES

TRANSLATED BY

REGINALD MAXWELL WOOLLEY, D.D.

Canon of Lincoln and Rector of Minting

LONDON

SOCIETY FOR PROMOTING CHRISTIAN KNOWLEDGE
NEW YORK AND TORONTO: THE MACMILLAN CO.
1930

PRINTED IN INDIA
BY NORMA ROGE
AT THE DIOCESAN PRESS, MADRAS, 1930. C9820

INTRODUCTION

THE Church of Egypt claims to have derived its faith
from the preaching of St. Mark the Evangelist, and the
long line of Patriarchs of Alexandria count him the first
in the line of succession.

To the average Englishman, the Egyptian or Coptic
Church is little more than a name, but it is in many
ways the most interesting of the 'separated' Eastern
Churches, that is, of those ancient Eastern Churches
which, for one reason or another, are not in communion
with the Orthodox Church of the East.

In ancient days the Egyptian Church produced some of
the greatest names in the history of the Church. Among
them may be counted Clement, the famous head of the
great School of Alexandria, Origen, Dionysius, the
'Isapostolic' Athanasius, and certainly not least among
scholars and theologians, the vigorous and masterful
patriarch Cyril. The name of Cyril is peculiarly
identified with Egypt. He is the great Egyptian saint,
and the Liturgy in common use to this day is the one that
is ascribed to, or at least named after, him.

The Copts are monophysites, and are in communion
with the monophysite Churches of Syria and Armenia.
On the other hand, the Coptic Church, by reason of the
geographical situation of Egypt and its long isolation
from the rest of the Christian East, is perhaps more than
any other Eastern Church, what we should call a national
Church.

As has been said, the Coptic Church is monophysite.
To understand its position in this respect, it is necessary

to take a short survey of the great theological controversies which rent the Christian Church from the time of
the Council of Nicea in 325, till the condemnation of
Eutyches at the Council of Chalcedon in 451.

The series of great theological controversies which
shook the Church to its foundation began with the
heresy of Arius. Arius taught that the Divine Son was
a creature, and that there was a time when he had not
yet been created. And it followed, though it was only
the followers of Arius who logically developed his
teaching in this direction, that the Holy Ghost was also
created. In effect this was teaching tritheism, a
supreme God, the Father, and two lesser and subject
deities, the Son and the Holy Ghost.

The Church had never hitherto actually defined the
relations of the Divine Persons in the Holy Trinity.
She had been content with teaching One God in three
Persons, Father, Son, and Holy Ghost. It is true that
early writers had sometimes used language which,
pressed to a logical conclusion, would seem to imply a
subordination of the Person of the Son to the Father,
but such definite subordination as that taught by Arius
was recognized at once as new and false teaching.
Moreover, the danger of this teaching was much intensi-
fied by the fact that Arius embodied his doctrine in
hymns to popularize it among the unlettered classes.
The Council of Nicea, the first of the great General
Councils, was called in 325 to deal with the pressing
danger. There seems to have been very little difference
of opinion at the Council as to the falseness of the
teaching of Arius, but the difficulty of defining the true
doctrine of the Church soon became evident. At first an
attempt was made to put forward the Baptismal Creed of
the Church of Cæsarea as embodying the true faith.